Bonds
and
Betrayal

Book design by Alex P. Johnson

ISBN 13
978-1-63132-260-0
Library of Congress Control Number: 2025914262

Library of Congress Cataloging-in-Publication Data
is available upon request.

First Edition

Published in the United States of America by ALIVE Book Publishing
an imprint of Advanced Publishing LLC
3200 A Danville Blvd., Suite 204, Alamo, California 94507
alivebookpublishing.com

PRINTED IN THE UNITED STATES OF AMERICA

10 9 8 7 6 5 4 3 2 1

Bonds
and
Betrayal

Annette Moureu

ABOOKS

Alive Book Publishing

*I dedicate this book to all women
whose voices are waiting to be heard
and who need to break the bonds of abuse
today, tomorrow, and in the future.
To my daughters Cloe and Jenna,
I love you!
Thank you for keeping it real.*

Acknowledgment

I would like to acknowledge my advisor, counsel, and friend, Jessica, for listening to my story and journey and keeping the notes to share and put in book form. I thank Dion, an excellent massage therapist and writer. Thank you for our many meetings at Bakers Square that started it all, putting pen to paper and giving my journey a purpose and life.

Contents

Prologue

Our environment, our upbringing, and our genes shape our lives. Our early experiences create our beliefs about our identity, the people around us, and the world. We learn about emotional bonds early in life as our brains develop quickly from newborn to adulthood. Being raised in a positive environment affects us as we grow up to be happy, self-assured, and optimistic people.

Childhood trauma and oppression can poorly affect our outlook, personality, and relationships.

Being exposed to negative childhood experiences can cause us to have poor self-esteem and a lack of self-confidence.

Children develop expectations about their world and its people through how their parents fulfill their needs. A person can develop an insecure attachment style when their needs are not met as a child. As a result of abuse or neglect, children grow up feeling that they do not deserve love or care in a relationship. Parents who tend to micromanage their children's activities can create problems for children when they grow up. For example, children who are micromanaged by their parents often find it difficult to make choices in their adulthood. Therefore, they develop low self-esteem and possess little confidence in their own abilities.

In addition to the upbringing that we have received throughout our childhood, our DNA contains a biological memory of the stress, emotional deprivation, and hormones of our grandparents' generation as well as that of our great-grandparents. Research shows that a person's DNA may contain a biological memory of the stress that one's grandparents endured. This finding is called epigenetic inheritance. We are an accumulation of generations past.

I have a rare ability called 'hyperthymesia,' where I can recall many past experiences in great detail. This ability allows me to extensively recall the details of my life. I learned that people with hyperthymesia have difficulties letting go of painful events and traumatic memories that stay with them for life. My difficult childhood led to a series of negative adulthood experiences. Someone raised in an abusive or dysfunctional household often fails to escape the negative pattern even after adulthood.

It's important to heal the painful memories of the past. Learning more about our background can clear things up about ourselves. In my 40's, I developed uterine fibroids. That's when I began my long journey of healing. It was a powerful journey. I had acupressure done for fibroids. I did acupuncture and then abdominal massage. Then, I learned about the many physical conditions that exist for people and how they can heal their lives. I learned that fibroids could happen to women who are not being able to speak up. That was a turning point for me. I saw the connection between my physical health and my mental health.

I began to do an inventory and went to a counselor to look at my life. I joined a group called AATH (American Association of Therapeutic Humor). Therapeutic humor is about bringing humor back into our lives, which will have therapeutic benefits. In 1996, I became a member. I learned how important humor is for healing. That's when I became aware that fibroids were a direct message that the body gives us, which tells us that history is held in the body. I began to read daily meditations.

Helping people to heal can help us heal ourselves.

I became an RN in 1974. Years later, I became part of a pain management program in June of 1984. In the program, we did relaxation tapes with patients. I then realized that relaxation training was a missing piece in nursing and health care because relaxation is an important component in stress reduction.

Between 1987 and 1991, I traveled with doctors around the San Francisco Bay Area who were part of a local pain management program. From 1993-1995, I was a volunteer spokesperson for the Arthritis Foundation, and I spoke with different small arthritis support groups on pain management and stress reduction. During the period of 1996 through 2006, I spoke on stress reduction with the annual Girl Scout convention called Discovery in the East Bay. In 2001, I started my own business called The Relaxation Connection, where I helped my clients with pain management and stress reduction using acupressure and massage.

I hope that in writing my own story, I can be a conduit by helping others with their healing journey.

Chapter One

My Grandfather

It all starts at home. The shape of our character takes its root in our home. Our early experiences create our belief about our identity, the people around us, and the world in general. We learn about emotional bonds early in life as our brains develop quickly from newborn to toddlerhood. Being raised in a positive environment affects us positively as we grow up to be happy, self-assured, and optimistic. Positive childhood experiences reduce the likelihood of histrionic, sadistic, or narcissistic traits.

As a young girl, my cousins told me stories of abuse in the family. One of my cousins had done research on both sides of the family. She put a book together regarding the family's genealogy. We all knew that our grandfather, Patrick, was a San Francisco police officer in the 1900s. But before he became a policeman, he was a meticulous gardener. He worked at a very prominent family-owned estate. That's the same place where my grandfather ended up meeting my grandmother, Helen, who was the upstairs maid. They eventually got married, and my grandmother became a stay-at-home mom. They had twelve children, and my grandfather quit being a gardener to be a police officer.

Some men would choose to become police officers because they like to be in charge. As police officers, they need to assert their power. They are also tough and aggressive, which allows them to showcase their inherent characteristics. My cousin dug into the San Francisco Police Department's historical records and discovered a story that indicated my grandfather was "tough and aggressive." Patrick and his partner worked on the beat in the Embarcadero area of San Francisco. My cousin relayed that there used to be a ton of union problems with the longshoremen in the city at the time. One day, a man showed up at the Embarcadero Center and was unruly with my grandfather and his partner. He was suspected of being a part of the union problem. A brawl ensued between this man, my grandfather, and his partner. The duo roughed up this man, and he fled. Later, the two policemen went off to eat, and as they were heading back to their beat, the same troublemaker at the Embarcadero Center showed up and shot Patrick's partner.

Aggression ran in my family. As my grandfather was abusive, so was my father. As they say, like father, like son. My grandfather was abusive to his wife and children. Kids are like sponges; they absorb everything they see or hear. As my father grew up in a toxic household, he absorbed toxicity to the extent that he made it part of his personality. He became toxic himself. Being abused as a child made him an abuser in adulthood. Living with abuse impacts you emotionally and mentally. It affects the way you view relationships and treat people around you. My father grew up in abuse; he didn't know any better. His role model was my grandfather, who was the epitome of abuse and oppression. So, my father treated my mother and me as if he subconsciously acquired the same patterns from his father. It had a ripple effect. My mother and I endured his abuse silently. I was intimidated and discredited, and so was my mother. Somehow, I thought that I was the one to provoke my father's aggressive side as if I had done something wrong to deserve it. Seeing my mother suffer in silence taught me to stay quiet as well. I didn't know any better.

Growing up in an abusive and alcoholic household can lead to behavioral issues in children. Most times, they are affected subconsciously. They may look as fine as ever, but appearances can be deceiving. These children become so used to violence that they attract abusive partners as they get older because they are familiar with it. And familiarity can be comforting.

A similar thing happened to me as well. I ended up with an abusive partner. I also developed a fear of questioning wrongful actions due to the harsh environment that I grew up in. Since my voice was stifled as a kid, I always felt uncomfortable speaking up for my rights. I had a hard time saying no when, with all my heart, it pushed me to take a stand for myself. So, I'd become numb when my abusive partner would scold me.

Instead of questioning his behavior and putting my foot down, I would suffer. I would suffer silently like a caged bird forced to endure when she is meant to be free and fly with the wind. I would blame myself for his actions because I was made to think that I was the problem when, in fact, he was. He always was! He, like my father, would make me wrong to make himself right, and this would continue forever.

The amount of abuse I suffered as an adult mainly concerns the abuse that I endured in childhood. Perhaps I would have put an end to it faster if I had been raised a strong, independent girl with a voice of my own. Or if I were taught what abuse is and how wrong it is to abuse someone. I was always made to feel little. My wishes were always dismissed as if I were not an individual. This type of mistreatment affected me. My self-image was negative, and my self-worth was null. The physical and emotional abuse

damaged my personal values, so when I suffered it all over
again as an adult, I felt as if I deserved it. It was similar to
the abuse I received from my father during my formative
years. I was forced back into the cycle of abuse that I thought
I'd broken out of. It felt painstakingly familiar, being
wounded in the same spot over and over. Fear settled in my
heart. I always felt that everything was my fault and that I
would be blamed for everything that would go wrong
around me. It was the only feeling I knew in my formative
years, and then it was back with a bang (pun intended) in
my adulthood. Those who are usually abusive — emotionally or physically — never think they are abusive. The emotional abuse was as pervasive in my family as a generational
story passed down through families to children, grandchildren, and beyond. Could it be possible that we are an accumulation of our previous generations?

Chapter Two

Early Childhood

My father was not a pleasant man. He was an adamant disciplinarian. As far as I recall, I was 14 years old at the time of the incident. I was in my bedroom getting ready for a bath when my mother and I had a heated argument. I recall my father unexpectedly entering my bedroom with a belt in his hand. While my mother moved to the door frame, he began to beat me. She stood by as my father beat me while I was naked on my bed.

I recall lying on my left side while he was beating me. Looking up at him, I noticed an evil energy in his eyes. My mother entered the bedroom without saying anything after he had stopped. I entered the bathroom to prepare for my bath. Nobody said anything.

My father was a member of the Knights of Columbus and the Young Men's Institute (YMI). He was always devout and religious. To everyone, he sounded like Mr. Nice Guy, Mr. Pious. He pretended to be self-assured as if he had never done anything wrong. He frequently refused to accept responsibility for anything and would blame me because he believed that everything was always my fault, and I couldn't understand why. Instead of complimenting me when I did something good, he said, "You're smarter than I thought."

My father was constantly watching and criticizing me. He was the castle's king. If I pleased him, he would never say, "Good job." He was fond of saying, "You're smarter than I thought." He would verbally humiliate me if I did not please him. On the other hand, my mother always said how fortunate I was to be with them. "Wait until you go to the school of hard knocks; then, you'll really appreciate what you have," she'd say. She was always concerned that I would value my upbringing. My mother's constant focus gave me the impression that I was adopted.

This could imply that both my mother and father were not my biological parents. Oddly, there aren't any pictures of my mother holding me as an infant until I was three months old. In January 1998, my mother was officially diagnosed with dementia and Alzheimer's. My father died in October of 1998. When I called Uncle Jack to inform him that my father had died, my mother yelled at me, "That's my husband," as if she was correcting me by saying, "That's my husband, not your father."

My father's abuse and remarks indicated that I might not have been his real child. I was born in March of 1953, and the earliest pictures that I found of myself were in June of 1953. My baptism certificate was dated April 26, 1953, but I saw no pictures of that event. I often wonder who I was and who raised me between birth and June 1953. My mother told me that I was not breastfed because I did not want her milk. I was an only child.

I remember a white car pulling up and stopping outside my home when I was 12 years old. There were two couples in the car. A man in the back of the car asked me if I was Annette Moureu. The woman seated next to him leaned forward and looked me over with no expression. She appeared calm and seemed to be in her 30s. Ten years later, when I got married, I saw that woman again at my wedding. She sat in the back of the church. Looking back, that person could have been my biological mother, and I could have been adopted. This history has haunted me for a long time.

I went on a website called 23andMe, which provided me with an ancestry service where I could learn about my family's DNA and family tree. This was a gift that my daughters gave me for Christmas one year. When I got my report, I was surprised to find out it didn't seem to resonate with what my parents told me about their background. Several years later, I purchased a DNA kit from Ancestry.com. It seemed to be more accurate based on what my parents told me. It showed a few hits from different relations in the family. I only had some hits of my cousins. Upon studying this more and speaking to a friend, we realized that an indicator on the tree and blue dots were shown for the people I was related to. I did not have that with my mother and father. There was no indication that these people were my parents at base value.

Being exposed to domestic violence can wreak havoc in a child's life. Memories can remain in the unconsciousness of children and linger on with them as they become adults. Memories are rooted in the hippocampus of the brain. The hippocampus is involved in storing long-term memories and making those memories resistant to forgetting. Every word we speak, every action we take, and every decision we make is under observation. Children are learning life cues from everyone in their environment. Some children may seem lost in their own world, not caring about their surroundings, but in reality, they are observing everything. They take in everything they see or hear. It affects them in one way or another.

The memories of growing up under abuse and oppression have a strong way of affecting every aspect of our lives, forming our personalities and hurting our relationships. We find ourselves falling into pessimism, hopelessness, and an overwhelming sense of worthlessness when faced with the merciless grip of severe adverse experiences during our formative years. However, this is only the beginning of the grim reality; the effects of this suffering may go well beyond our early years. If left unattended, these wounds scab over and manifest as psychological or mental health issues that relentlessly follow us into adulthood.

Our early years are of utmost importance because, during this critical time, we establish the delicate bonds that will later determine our attachment style. Based on how our needs were met or not by our parents, it is through these early connections that we start to build our expectations about the world and its inhabitants. Unmet needs cause us to develop an insecure attachment style, which harms our relationships. The emotional turmoil we experience due to the scars left by childhood abuse or neglect can further throw us into a disjointed and disordered attachment.

Tragically, adults who exhibit these attachment patterns frequently believe that they are unworthy of affection or care in future relationships.

These unfortunate events result in serious difficulties that people must overcome as they navigate the complexities of adulthood. For instance, children whose parents micromanage frequently struggle with making decisions in their adult lives. They become the victims of self-doubt and uncertainty in their lives. They constantly lose faith in their abilities, severely damaging their self-worth. Similarly, unsupportive parents' lack of encouragement or support weighs heavily on their children.

My own story starts to take shape in the context of such trying circumstances. My adult experiences have been significantly impacted by the trials of a problematic childhood characterized by abuse and dysfunction. Unfortunately, the bad habits that developed during my upbringing have proven obstinately persistent, refusing to let go of their grip even as I started my adult life.

Even though I wished for a different reality, my early life was far from idyllic. My mother was born in 1914, and my father was born in 1906. They both married one another on November 3, 1951, and I was born on March 25, 1953.

My life was incorporated into this chaotic weaving by the struggles of a traumatic upbringing. As an only child, I had to carry the burden of my abusive upbringing without the comfort and company that having siblings might have offered. I could not express my emotions because my parents did not understand the importance of my needs and wants. Instead, they wanted me to become a nun and live a life of religious piety because it aligned with their desires and aspirations. They enrolled me in a Catholic school to further this vision, shaping my early course.

My Aunt Tessa, a presence who casts a gloomy shadow over my formative years, emerges from the shadows as I travel through the halls of my memories and trace the path of my childhood. She was my father's sister and had an arsenal of criticism, ridicule, and denigration. She didn't miss a chance to make me the target of her contempt, and when she did, the force of her rage tore through the delicate fabric of my self-worth. She created an atmosphere of humiliation with her constant presence and criticized me in front of others watching. She seemed to view me as always at fault and deserving of her continuous mockery.

One particular memory serves as a menacing reminder of the darkness I experienced. I remember when my Aunt Tessa babysat me when I was approximately three years old.

I have a memory of walking into a bedroom and seeing my Uncle Elmer lying in a bed. He sat up on the side of the bed and asked me to come over to him. I remember him pushing my head downward into his lap. At that moment, Aunt Tessa entered the room suddenly, grabbed my right arm, and pulled me out of the room. She then shouted at me, "We don't tell on Daddy!" These words would reverberate in my soul forever.

These words, which became ingrained in my being, served as the chains that restrained my cries for justice and bound me to secrecy. After that horrifying incident, Aunt Tessa's rage knew no bounds. She inflicted a cruel punishment on me that was both physical and psychological, leaving me scarred, speechless, and burdened by the weight of my secret truth.

These suppressed memories finally broke through in the crucible of adulthood as the sands of time continued their relentless flow. "We don't tell on Daddy," was whispered to me, and those words continued reverberating inside me, emerging in unexpected ways and casting a shadow over my relationships and perception of myself. Even within the sacred walls of my marriage, my actions and beliefs were influenced by the scars of my past, which had woven a tangled web.

Chapter Three

Courtship With Husband Taylor

My father was not very nice to me over the years. He was often very critical of me. There were never any conversations asking me how I was doing. Most of the time, he would only criticize me, and he constantly pushed me to go to church and other avenues related to church. I remember he wanted me to go to the novenas at church. He never encouraged me to find my passion, go to college, or pursue any career I would be interested in. He never asked me how my life was going. He never stood up for me in any way. This basically led to me being stifled in my growth. I was so used to this kind of treatment that I ended up with an abusive partner.

In the summer of 1971, I became a USO junior volunteer. I enjoyed it a lot. During that time, the country was winding down from the Vietnam War. Dating was not easy for me when I was growing up. I went to an all-girls high school, which I enjoyed, but I did not date during that time. I did not have any brothers or a lot of male friends. I enjoyed the USO experience because I met men from all over the country. During that time, I went to City College after high school. My friends and I went to dances and talks and group events. I was working at the USO canteen, and during this time, I met Taylor. I was very attracted to him because he reminded me of my favorite cousin, Pete. Taylor had blond hair and glasses. He was easy-going, mild, kind, and respectful. He seemed nice enough.

On our first date, he visited me at my San Francisco

home. I was 18 years old when we were dating, and Taylor would start discussing marriage immediately. I felt pushed and anxious because I didn't know him well enough. We had a few dates. I was busy in school. I found it strange that Taylor gave my telephone number to another man. At that time, Taylor and I had a date, and he canceled on me because he told me that his grandfather Pete had a heart attack and he had to go back to Minnesota to be with him. Then I got this call from his friend who wanted to go on a date with me. I declined because I didn't know this man. I didn't particularly appreciate that Taylor did not show respect for me by giving my phone number to another man without discussing it with me.   Taylor later told me that he had lied to me and that he just wanted to go hunting with his grandfather. School was my life, and I was too busy to date Taylor a lot anyway. We began dating in the summer of 1971. When I met Taylor, he was in the Navy and on a ship called the USS Ranger. The ship was in a dry dock, preparing to go to Vietnam. Because of the Vietnam War controversy, the ship remained at Hunter's Point Naval Shipyard in San Francisco. It was in dry dock for another year.

Then, in approximately a year or two, Taylor left the country for Vietnam. He was responsible for sending ammunition to wherever they needed to be shipped. During that period, we communicated a lot with one another by mail. When he returned, the ship was based in the naval air station in Alameda.

We continued our friendship, and we casually dated. At one time, we planned to go on a date, and he tripped and broke his leg. He ended up in Oaknole Hospital for a while. My mother and father took me to visit him while he was at the hospital. After being released from the hospital, he did shore duty at Treasure Island. Later, he was transferred to Tacoma, Washington, and worked on a destroyer called the USS Orleck. We stayed connected through telephone calls and letters.

By June 1974, I graduated from nursing school and began my first RN job. This decision met with some complexities due to my father's initial desire for me to become a nun. Despite the familial pressure, I opted for nursing, and as a newbie, I chose to work evening shifts.

Living at home during this period, my parents supported me in my evening shifts. They graciously drove me to and from work. During those months, from October to January, they would pick me up at midnight, and during these rides, they would inform me that Taylor had called that night. Though seemingly odd, this routine became a recurrent piece in the unfolding narrative.

In October 1974, Taylor came to visit me when his ship returned. During this time, my feelings for him were growing. I vividly recall sharing that I had developed emotions for Taylor with a friend. On that day, we went to Sausalito, a memory I can delve into for more details. We encountered Lois, a neighbor from my parents' block, during the visit. Taylor's behavior became peculiar as we headed downtown, planning to take the bus to the Embarcadero and then a ferry to Sausalito.

Upon our return, we went to my parents' house and had dinner. The details of the dinner are a bit hazy for me. Afterward, I borrowed their car so Taylor and I could converse at the beach. In a nutshell, I secretly hoped for our relationship to progress, perhaps to become more serious. I was unsure about Taylor's Navy status and station details, and I couldn't be sure about his specific assignment in Alameda

or later in Tacoma, Washington. Nevertheless, when he returned, stationed either in Alameda or Tacoma, we engaged
in conversations about various topics.

Suddenly, Taylor took an unexpected turn in the conversation, confessing, "I'm not the person you think I am. I have
a temper." In addition to this, he said some other things that
weren't nice. I don't particularly remember those things that
were said, but his tone is imprinted on my mind, which was-
n't nice. Along with this, he kept making excuses.

This revelation marked a significant shift in our interac-
tion and left me pondering the true nature of the person I
thought I knew. Reflecting on the events, I acknowledge the
natural progression of emotions when getting to know
someone over time. I did not understand the dynamics of
abuse and manipulation then. I wasn't aware of the cycle
where victims attract abusers themselves, and similarly,
abusers are drawn to victims as well. I felt this was one of
those cases.

Despite my hopes for a blossoming relationship, Taylor
initiated the breakup, which he eventually did. This revelation took me by complete surprise, prompting me to consider seeking hypnosis to unlock the buried memories of
that momentous event.

Reflecting on the breakup years later, I discovered an in-
triguing piece of the puzzle that shed light on the involve-
ment of Taylor's mother. But at that time, It was just my
speculation.

I suspected that his mother played a significant role in
the dissolution of our relationship. I speculated that Taylor
may have mentioned our relationship to his mother during
casual conversations. This must have triggered her to devise
a plan to discourage our connection. This suspicion is

supported by the fact that prior to that visit, everything seemed fine, with us exchanging letters in January and December of 1973.

This interference became evident when, in June of 1974, Taylor's brother Arthur was marrying Lisa. Twenty years later, I saw a photo of Taylor and his brother Parker holding a line of fish. This photo was taken during a visit to his family. It was more about me seeing him with the fish, in that picture with his brothers, all appearing happy. So years later, while looking at the picture, I realized that Taylor was there in Minnesota in June 74 when his brother got married, and after that, he came to meet me in October of 74 and gave me concern. I was unsure where he was stationed in between, so it made me wonder if something had happened in between. Things seemed fine before he left for the wedding in '74. I had suspicions that Taylor's mother could have a controlling and interfering nature.

The suspicion of Taylor's mother's interference added a layer of complexity to the breakup. It left me with lingering questions about the true motivations behind his decision. Her interference was evident throughout our marriage as well.

Chapter Four

Meeting Taylor's Family

Once Taylor was out of my life, I became involved with my work as a new RN. I worked the evening shift at a local hospital. I enjoyed my work. It was a challenging year; hence, seeking solace, I went to visit my friend Susie and her mom, Jo Nell, in Texas. Their supportive efforts aimed to help me navigate the aftermath of the breakup, offering comfort during a challenging period. Susie and her mom, both now passed, were integral parts of my life. I grew up with Susie on the block, where she had a family with two brothers, a mom, and a dad. The neighborhood was pleasant, but eventually, her parents divorced, and she moved to Texas with her mother.

I made it through with help from my friends, and within the first year, my colleagues at work encouraged me to leave home and get my place. In April 1975, I bought my first car and moved into my apartment in September 1975. That year, I never contacted Taylor, and we never talked. He wrote a letter to my parents' home, which was forwarded to me in my apartment, which I received in Sep/Oct. In the letter, he wrote, "You wouldn't marry me last year, but would you marry me now?"

I thought he was either drunk when he wrote it or, looking back, he might have had some encounter with his brother and sister-in-law or maybe his mother. I couldn't confidently say what had happened, but something happened. Over the years, his mother seemed overly protective and intrusive. In addition to this, Arthur and his wife Lisa seemed very cool toward me and not too accepting of me marrying his brother. I couldn't figure out why.

When I received Taylor's letter while he was living with his parents, I told him we needed to talk. When he called me, I asked him if what he told me back in 1974 was a pack of lies. He didn't respond; he sort of grunted. I invited him to San Francisco, and he stayed with me. We went out to dinner with my parents, went to the wine country, and enjoyed our time together. During one instance in my apartment, I tried to hug him, but he pushed me away. I couldn't understand why we couldn't be closer.

During his stay, we discussed his original marriage proposal in his letter. While discussing this, he suddenly told me he changed his mind about getting married. This shocked me because he did this the last time we were together in 74, when he changed his mind, telling me he was not a good guy. This time, he wrote me a letter proposing marriage, flying out to San Francisco to be with me and then changing his mind again. I started to cry because I was stunned by his actions, and then he said, "Okay, let's get married." For a moment, I felt maybe I didn't want to get married to a person like Taylor. I thought it was time for me to be open-minded and appreciative of what was in front of me and say "Yes to love."

I had reservations about getting married. I felt we were different people and wanted to wait at least a year to see if we still had anything in common. I had finished school and started working while he had been to war, and I never thought about how it might have affected him with PTSD. That's important because If I had been more aware of PTSD, I might have considered, *Well, Taylor just got out of the service. This might not be the best time for marriage.* It's akin to when people enter recovery for alcohol or drug addiction, and they are advised against entering a relationship for a certain period. Despite all this, I finished school and got a job.

The crying person was a little girl scared not to have a man, but an adult stepped in momentarily, thinking, *"Oh, maybe we don't have to get married."* This is what I said and convinced myself, *"This is your chance, Marie, this is what you want. I always back pedal."*

I took The EST seminar training in 74. It helped me understand my hesitancy or back peddling, indecisiveness, and fear. To provide more context, Erhard Seminars Training, Inc. was an organization founded by Werner Erhard in 1971 that offered a two-weekend (6-day, 60-hour) course known officially as "The Est Standard Training." The purpose of the training is to help one recognize that the situations that seem to be holding them back in life are working themselves out within the process of life itself. After the seminar, I felt a little better, and part of me thought I didn't date enough men. Once, Taylor and I had a discussion about marriage, and he told me, "You dated a lot of men. What's wrong with you? Why aren't you ready?" That was one of the biggest red flags. However, I did date several guys in 1974/1975 when Taylor and I were separate. I always, in some way, missed Taylor. Taylor called his family in Minnesota, asked about living arrangements, and said, "I finally convinced her to move to Minnesota."

What intention guided his return to get me? It wasn't a mere happenstance at this point. I would assert that there was a plan in motion, unbeknownst to me. Perhaps his mother and family played a role. I say 'perhaps' because, truthfully, I did not have all the details at that time. However, something felt amiss. I questioned it, but my understanding went no further than that.

We finished our visit, talked about getting married, and then he left a day or two later. I remember my friend Jenny visiting me after Taylor left and telling her the news.

November 1975

The first time I flew out to meet Taylor's family, we got stuck in a ditch. It was a bad sign. It had been snowing when he picked me up from the Fargo airport, and instead of heading straight over to his parental home, we went to his brother Arthur and his wife Lisa, where I would stay. What a welcome! They greeted me in hunting gear. I had the strangest feeling but put it aside. I could have just been nervous, but in my gut, I knew things to be a bit odd. Here I am, a city girl from San Francisco, and my husband's family are hunters.

Before visiting Arthur and Lisa, we stopped somewhere, and Taylor gave me the engagement ring. When I arrived at Arthur and Lisa's house, it was a typical farmhouse with lots of open space around it. I saw part of Taylor's family sitting on the couch. The first one was Arthur, Taylor's brother. The second person was Lisa, Arthur's wife. The third person was Taylor's father, Conrad. They just all looked at me and were not very conversational. They had gone hunting that day. Because it was near the holidays, I brought a fruit cake for Arthur and Lisa. Taylor's father left. He didn't say much to me when I joined the family as the years went on. Taylor showed me the room, and I talked with Arthur and Lisa a little bit and got ready for bed. Taylor went back to his home, which was the farm.

The next day, Taylor took me to breakfast at his home in Brandon, where Arthur and Lisa lived. His family were farmers. He took me home to meet his mother and the rest of his family. I met his mother, Tracy. His mother, Tracy, reminded me of Aunt Tessa. She seemed friendly enough, but I was skeptical of how she noticed my engagement ring and took my hand to look at it. Taylor went to work with his father in the barn. We talked a bit about different things, and Taylor came up for lunch with Conrad, and I got to speak with them. Taylor was the eldest of six in the family. His second brother, Arthur, lived nearby with his wife, Lisa. The third oldest brother was Parker, who lived in Wahpeton, North Dakota.

Taylor also had three younger siblings, Josie, Jacob, and Mateo. Josie was about 12, Jacob was about 10, and Mateo was about 8. Jean, Jacob, and Mateo were in school. They came home later in the afternoon. I was sitting in the front room while Tracy was cleaning the kitchen. First, Jacob pops into the front room. He had red hair. The second one to come in was Josie. She had dark brown hair. The third person to come into the front room was Mateo. Mateo had curly blonde hair with a black hoodie. When I saw Mateo's face, I thought it was Taylor. The kids hurried off to put their things away. I went to talk to Tracy in the kitchen. I told her about Mateo, who was sixteen years younger than Taylor. Mateo looked a lot like Taylor. Taylor was the firstborn. Mateo was the sixth birth. I asked Tracy, "If you had a 7th child, would they look like the second child, Arthur?" Tracy did not say a word and just nodded. I never told anybody, but from then on, Tracy was not very warm to me throughout our marriage. I thought I would give the family a chance. I respected their journey. I didn't see anything abnormal at the time. I stayed with Arthur and Laurie for about a week and interacted with the family.

The next day, Tracy approached me and said, "Taylor said he wants to marry a woman he could control, and I would bring him back to the Blessed Virgin Mary." I found that to be an uncomfortable communication issue. As time went on, I suspected and thought that maybe she could be intimidating, manipulative, challenging, and cruel to me and other members of the family, but I wasn't certain. Years down the line, I found something useful as well, which was that the eldest daughter of Arthur and Lisa, among the two daughters they had, was diagnosed with a major disease, "Cerebral Palsy." In addition to this, her mother Lisa was even abusive towards her as well.

December 1975:

I eventually went back to my work in San Francisco. Taylor and I kept in contact because we were engaged. He came down to visit again in December 1975 and stayed two weeks. Something changed. We did not feel as emotionally connected as we had in previous times. It was the same response as 74 when he visited his mother and family. Possibly, there were questions about our relationship. We ended up both going to talk with a priest about getting married in April. Taylor did something odd. We were discussing, and he seemed irritable, and all of a sudden, he said, "I'm tired of waiting; let's go and set a date." His behavior was odd. He returned to Minnesota at the end of December; we were not emotionally involved from then on.

The revelation that puzzled me for years was Taylor's sudden desire to get married. The lingering question that bothered me for decades was, *"Why was he in a hurry to get married by April?"* Although I didn't give enough thought before we got married or even as years went down the road. It was not until, after two to three years, Taylor died that I began to review our whole relationship. One of the pieces was, *"Why did he write me that letter in 75 to get married? What happened?"*

I later discovered that Lisa was about four months pregnant as well. I also noticed Mateo, who was 16 years younger, had a strong resemblance to Taylor.

In a casual conversation, Tracy (Taylor's mother) shared an unsettling revelation. This disclosure shed light on Taylor's mindset, indicating a controlling and religious aspect I was unaware of.

This significant information added depth to the narrative, offering insights into Taylor's intentions and attitudes toward marriage. It explained the perplexing question that had haunted me for decades, providing a clearer understanding of the dynamics involved during that period of my life.

Looking back, the puzzle pieces fell into place. It was November, and Lisa, Taylor's sister-in-law, was four months pregnant. Counting backward from November, we land in August. It was the same month when Taylor sent me that perplexing letter. I suspected something might have happened between Taylor and Lisa due to the timing of the letter and the fact that both were known for heavy drinking, but certainty eludes me.

In addition to this, Taylor was grappling with PTSD at that time as well after leaving the Navy. It was a fact that he spent a considerable amount of time with Lisa and Arthur. The alcohol-fueled environment might have led to some questionable hookups, with Lisa becoming pregnant or maybe not. All of these things were my suspicions, and there were many elements of uncertainty, and I wasn't sure of what I was suspecting.

I was suspicious when Taylor wrote me a letter asking if I would marry him now. Taylor's impulsive behavior was a recurring pattern that raised questions. On the contrary, when we met in October, he seemed unsure about marriage, showing signs of being on the fence. He was running from something, contemplating a union with me as a test.

Between January 1, 1976, and March 1976, we were on and off again about getting married for the third time. Even after he committed and went through the trouble of contacting me again, he backpedaled again about getting married.

Did something happen between Taylor and Laurie?

Did he want to marry me or someone else?

Did he even want to marry a man?

The answers to all these questions eluded me until Taylor eventually got me. But at that point, I would have said to myself if I were clear-headed, "Marie, this is not a good relationship. It's not meant to be. Cut the cord and get back to your life. You will be okay".

We kept in contact. He continued working on the farm and even looked for other means of work to support us. He was having a hard time getting to work. This was another red flag, but I just figured these weren't easy times, and he had just gotten out of the service. It was the Midwest, and after the holidays, too. He wrote that in a letter to me, and I felt we wouldn't be rushing into a marriage after all.

January 1976:

In early January, after the new year, Taylor had called me in panic and were shooting all these questions like, "What do you want from me?" He said, "Do you want to get married or not? When do you want to get married?"

I replied, "We wanted to get married in April. I mentioned to Taylor, "If you don't want to marry, that's okay. We don't have to get married."

I called the priest and canceled the wedding plans. After that, I found out later that the day Taylor called, he was angry, had been drinking, and had also visited his brother Arthur. Then it hit me again that whenever he visited his family, the same reaction occurred from his side with all the questions while making me look bad.

This was a person who was trying to hide something. The family may or may not know about something, but he made me the one who was at fault every time. Around the same time, a new development happened: Lisa delivered Joy in January. She was premature for one month, so how could that be? When I talked to Jennie, she told me years later that she was a month early and due in February.

In January of 1976, I visited Taylor and his family for the second time. I stayed with Taylor's grandfather, Pete. Tracy, Taylor's mother, wasn't too warm towards me, and I did not know why. When I was up there, he was working on the farm and said, "If you did not come to visit me in January, I was going to call the wedding off." What an arrogant thing to say. He acted as if he were the only one in charge of this critical decision or as if he was the only one who was getting married. During that time, we put the wedding on hold. He was having a difficult time getting work outside the farm.

I returned home after staying with Taylor's grandfather for a few days. He called me one day during that time frame. I was home sick from work, and he told me that he wanted to reenlist in the Navy, and he was on his way to the Navy recruitment in Fargo, North Dakota. We talked about it and decided to continue putting the wedding on hold. He eventually decided to go back to school in Wahpeton, North Dakota. Somewhere in February, when he started school, he asked me how the wedding plans were coming along.

I reminded him, "Taylor, we put the wedding on hold. Do you still want to get married?"

He told me, "Yes."

Once again, we found ourselves backpedaling. Nevertheless, we plunged headfirst into it. So, by the time I thought, *Okay, let me pick up the ball again,* and visited him near my birthday in March, we had already entered wedding planning mode. Once more we found ourselves immersed in wedding plan mode. His behavior was cold and distant to me when we went to visit his family.

Taylor lived in Brandon, Minnesota, and went to school in Wahpeton, North Dakota, two border towns. Besides this, we visited his folks in Brandon, Minnesota, and Tracy was cool towards me; she gave me a cake, and a gift of sweater. When the two of us were in California, our connections were much more profound. Still, whenever we were in the presence of his hometown, there was an immediate river of distance between us, and nothing about us felt connected over the years. In fact, on my birthday, when he asked about wedding plans, I told him I could feel he did not love me and was very rude to me, after which I left devasted.

Additionally, my parents got on board with the wedding strangely and were very supportive. One of the nicest things my mom did was drive downtown and pick me up from the airport upon my return, which was a huge effort on her part and a big gesture. But at the same time, I was devasted because Taylor wasn't acting nice.

There will always be things about my husband that I may never understand, but that is true with anyone in any relationship. But then, there has always been that feeling that part of me never felt like I knew Taylor. My insight is that he was up to something and I didn't know what.

Chapter Five

Marriage Or Misery

June 1976: Our wedding day. In San Francisco, we made our promises to each other. Following the wedding, my groom and I headed for a honeymoon in Carmel. It was a little getaway from the whole world. I was relieved that some family members from Taylor's side had added the touch of home to the festivities. As we went from one round of visiting to the next in our bubble of newlywed bliss, they stuck around to visit with friends in California.

So, coming back from the honeymoon was a reality check. The feeling of carrying the luggage of our lives into the new place seemed overwhelming; after all, it was only three days of marital bliss. On second thought, maybe we had been given too much in one go. Yet, out of that chaos, Taylor's controlling tendencies floated like a dark cloud over the first few days of married life.

Our very first heated marital conflict was over something that seemed so small. I needed to pack my nursing school books and papers for future reference, but Taylor's reaction was anything but small. This idea made him angry, and I felt once more like a powerless child and gave in to his demands. With an ongoing pattern in which his dominance reigned, I was left feeling tiny and impotent in our relationship.

This was only the tip of the iceberg. This is the sign and symptom of a narcissist. Taylor escalated his behavior into intimidation tactics which made me feel battered physically and emotionally. His insistence on his way with explosive outbursts, brought out a subordination atmosphere in our marriage. Even when I tried to stick to my guns and stand my ground, it was only some time before I found myself capitulating under the full force of that great tower of strength.

Then, with the slow settling in of married life, the cracks within the relationship deepened, baring the darknesses that lay beneath. Taylor was very dismissive of my independence and began letting me have a bit of control, such as warning signs of defiance. This was growing clearer with each passing day. The idyllic picture of marriage I painted was coming apart at the seams, replaced by a real one that was more tense and insecure.

After marriage, we moved to Breckenridge, Minnesota, where Taylor pursued a course in restaurant management at the North Dakota State School of Science, and I took up work at St. Francis Hospital. In the meantime, Taylor got a job at the Breckenridge Standard Gas Station. We were, in fact, going in different directions in this new chapter of our lives.

The transition was by no means smooth. The grueling days of driving to our new home were to be followed by a rush to unload our belongings and then travel straight through to his family farm. In fact, any hopes of reprieve were thoroughly dashed as, at every turn, we were whisked along, leaving little time for the simple pleasures of settling in and getting used to our new surroundings.

Living in Minnesota only worsened the mystery that had clouded our marriage. Our social life seemed to be within the bounds or limits of his family, with only a few excursions from the norm. As each day passed, the very boundaries of our existence seemed to crowd in on us, and I found myself nodding to his wishes, as I was too afraid of what would happen if I dared say no. Defying him translated into inviting his wrath. This was something I learned the hard way very early on in my married life.

Our most intimate moments had become a battleground, sex a weapon of control that was doled out according to whim. In them, I was feeling more like a possession than a partner. His words cut deeper than any physical blow, leaving scars that ran far beyond the surface.

At this early time in our marriage, I felt that all independence was gone and had been replaced by ownership that could only render me powerless and trapped. What was first a relationship with so much promise had dissolved into a cycle of manipulation and coercion to where I found myself wondering if I would ever see the view of who I was again.

He did not say anything; he was quiet and kept to himself. A wife could cope with that, but that didn't last for long.

My husband could have been an actor with the Jekyll and Hyde role he played to a tee. In his quiet spells, things were peaceful and tolerable, but still, his silence was menacing. Or, he would swing through the door, reach into the fridge, and sit down in his chair. I had to go by my gut feelings and figure out what he wanted to keep him this way. That was by far the worst—trying to deal with the human element. It was nerve-wracking. If I did the slightest thing wrong or made an incorrect assumption, all hell broke loose, and, of course, it would be my fault. My fault. It was my fault, no matter what the rules were: if it was wrong, cost too much, didn't make sense, or was a bit off-kilter, it was all on me. The no-fault rule applied to my husband, Taylor. If the account was overdue, God forbid a bill was sent late—both were my fault. And if, somehow, anything his mother had to say when she called bugged him, that was also on me. If there was a family function that we couldn't make because of work, a sick child, or bad weather, that was all my fault. This was the invisible line that I was not allowed to cross, questions I was not allowed to ask, and strange encounters that unsettled me about relations within his family. I was to keep my mouth shut and not go start a bunch of crap that nobody wanted to hear about in the first place.

It was always this way: "At the drop of a hat" or "at a mere suggestion," we were headed back. "Moving back," and ended up at the family farm. There must have been an odd, twisted sense of comfort for him there. I say odd because I could even see he wasn't gung-ho about being there, but that is exactly what he did. We were blind, unsure, and doing the right thing. But there was the silent, nervous intuition that clinched at my innards, which I was told to be "silly nonsense."

His parents lived an hour from us in Brandon, Minnesota. We spent most of our free time up there. In some places in the Midwest, it was a tradition for the groomsmen to come and whisk away the bride. However, it did not happen because we were married in CA. When we were visiting the farm one day, later in the evening, Taylor's brothers, Parker and Arthur, came to their parent's home and took me for drinks at the local bar. They let me get my purse before they took me away! It was rather amusing getting to know them, although I wished that I had been warned beforehand. Even though my husband was aware of the tradition, he gave no hints at all that something like this would happen. He was acting aloof and distant that day. Much later, I realized he had been snarky during the whole time I had been with his brothers. Yet again, I kept wondering what on earth I had done.

I was trying to fit in and spend time with his family. The time I spent with them led to another problem. During the first three months, we were married and used to visit the farm; every time I would come back from the car, he would scold me for the comments his parents made about me. He thought he had no say over me. He also told me they wanted to know when I would return to work and why he couldn't control his wife.

The story continues in further parts, but here is a perfect place to reflect on the events that happened until this point. Win, lose, or draw, but I grew up in a house where the son of an abusive and violent father raised me. This set the trajectory for me to marry a man with the same name as my father, who was also abusive to me and who followed the same pattern in my life. Reflecting on my experiences, I see a clear and painful pattern of abuse and control that has spanned generations.

This journey has helped me become painfully aware of how our world, upbringing, and maybe even our DNA control our actions. This idea is at the core of epigenetic inheritance: if our ancestors were deprived emotionally, traumatized in some way, or stressed due to their environments, then those experiences are literally imprinted onto our DNA, impacting how we behave and react towards life.

It led to who I married with similar destructive patterns. My painful history of relationship violence is a glaring example that if I'm not careful and intentional, these trends will repeat without end.

Healing and release from these patterns continue with a realization of these inherited traits, leading to new and deliberate choices. It is important to not just learn from our history but try to take steps in advance so that we are able to prevent the same future from repeating itself.

After closing this chapter, I feel full of strength and hope. I hope that sharing my story will show anyone who might feel stuck in a change/release cycle like the one I experienced some light at the end of the tunnel. You are allowed to escape and heal in a better way, one that leaves a heritage of love and respect rather than pain and abuse. This process of understanding our history, learning from it, and moving beyond the status quo is vital. We can all reframe our stories and, in turn, be a model for future generations.

*

Chapter Six

Retreat And Repeat

Taylor and I were in the throes of young love when we were first married. Our apartment building's manager once called us because of the daily ruckus. The noise was from Taylor chasing me around our tiny apartment, tickling me until I submitted to his advances. In those first six months of our marriage, we were intimate several times a week. Not that I was always a willing participant, but I was the dutiful wife, submitting to his wishes to keep him happy. It felt like watching a ball of string unwinding and rewinding itself repeatedly.

Taylor was persistent, constantly pushing me verbally, emotionally, and mentally until he got his way. It seemed that sex was his way of easing tensions and keeping a semblance of a smile on his face. I believe the noise of our bed banging against the wall disturbed our neighbors. I wanted to apologize, but Taylor insisted they mind their business.

Back then, I liked him more, and I was genuinely under the impression that he liked me. Not just liked me but loved me, and perhaps he couldn't keep his hands off me because he found me irresistible. As the years went by, the world had a strange way of showing the truth. All that bed-banging may not have had anything to do with my sex appeal. It was more about his need to eliminate memories that haunted him.

I started to believe that Taylor was trying to erase something deeper. Perhaps he thought that having more sex would wash away the memories and feelings he desperately wanted to forget. His nightly six-pack of beer didn't help either. It was a cheap band-aid for a wound that needed deep, intense therapy. His pain spilled into our small family, and I had to face the ugly truth in ways I wasn't prepared for.

Those early years were a confusing mix of love and obligation. I wanted to believe that Taylor's affection for me was real. I hoped that our physical connection meant something deeper. But now, with the clarity of hindsight, I see it was more about his struggles than our bond.

Taylor's conduct reflected his inner struggle. His need to dominate and control me was a result of his unresolved concerns. While playing the role of loyal wife, I gradually lost myself. It's terrible to acknowledge, but our marriage was constructed on weak ground. The fissures were always present, hiding beneath the surface. As time passed, the gaps deepened, and the reality became more difficult to deny.

I wish I had noticed the signals sooner. I wish I had recognized that love should not come at the price of one's self-worth and dignity. But in those early years, I was too focused on making Taylor happy, too absorbed with the need to make our marriage work. Reflecting on such events, I have realized the importance of self-awareness and self-worth. In addition to this, I realized that true love is built on mutual respect and understanding.

It was October 1976, and I discovered I was pregnant. Taylor and I relocated to a mobile home the next year, just before Cloe was born. We resided on the campus where Taylor attended school. Living on campus had its perks, but it also meant we were isolated from family and friends. I often felt lonely and unsupported. Taylor was consumed with his studies and rarely had time for me or the baby. I struggled to balance motherhood with the demands of being a supportive wife.

However, when I was eight months pregnant with Cloe, our first child, I recall a critical occurrence - as if it had happened yesterday. One day, Taylor and I were watching TV together. Out of nowhere, he changed the channel without saying anything. Feeling a rare surge of defiance, I switched it back. We kept switching the TV channel back and forth. On the last switch, he grabbed me under my arms, pulled me away from the TV, and dragged me down the hallway to our bedroom.

I was yelling, "Taylor, Taylor, please let me go. Please put me down!" He didn't listen. He kept dragging me until he finally dumped me on the ground. I went to the bathroom and then went to bed. I didn't talk to him about it for a while. My memory of that night is still fuzzy.

Cloe was born in July of 1977. Her arrival brought a mix of joy and exhaustion. Being a new mother was overwhelming, but I loved Cloe wholeheartedly. Taylor was a proud father, but his behavior remained unpredictable.

But The incident with the TV was a turning point for me. It was the first time I truly felt afraid of Taylor. His anger and physical aggression were unlike anything I had experienced before. There were some shades during the course of the relationship, but this time, the intensity of his anger and aggression had increased. I began to see glimpses of a darker side of him, one that I couldn't ignore.

Despite the challenges, there were some moments of happiness. Cloe's first smile, her first laugh, and her first steps were the milestones that brought light and joy into my life. Events like these gave me the strength to keep going. But I started to question my marriage more often. I wondered if this was the life I wanted for Cloe and me. The love I once felt for Taylor had become an amalgamation of fear and uncertainty. There was a growing tension between us, but I didn't know how to address it.

Taylor's behavior got increasingly irregular as the months passed. One moment, he was the most attentive and affectionate person, and the next moment, he became aloof and rude. I never knew what to anticipate. I was walking on eggshells, trying to avoid anything irritating him.

One evening, I put Cloe to bed, and then I sat down and thought about all that had transpired in detail. Memories of our early days together, the TV incident, and our daughter's birth. I realized I needed to find a strategy to protect Cloe and me from Taylor's erratic actions.

I didn't have all the answers at that time, but I knew one thing: I couldn't keep living in terror. I had to have the courage to speak up for myself and make the best decisions for my kid and me. It was a terrifying concept, but I knew I needed to begin somewhere. One day, as I looked at Cloe sleeping happily, I made a silent pledge to her and myself. I would do my best to provide her with a secure and loving home. I would find a way to help her handle the trials ahead and grow up feeling safe and valued.

The path would not be simple, and I knew there would be difficult choices. But, for Cloe's sake, I was prepared to face anything that came our way. The events of October 1976 and the following months were only the start of a long and difficult journey. I was resolved to travel this journey with courage and resilience.

In those early days, fitting in often meant keeping quiet. Taylor and his friends and family would get cases and cases of beer and a few kegs and have gatherings where I was expected to sit quietly. At first, I tried to stay on the sidelines, but eventually, I grabbed a bottle for myself, desperately trying to smooth things over. Having a beer now and then made it easier to blend in.

Taylor graduated from school in March 1978. We packed our belongings and traveled cross-country back to California, staying with my parents until we found a place to live in Daly City. It was a hard moment. I got work at Seton Hospital, but Taylor struggled to find a consistent position in the food industry. He hopped about between professions, attempting to establish his foothold.

As the months passed, we attempted to settle into our new routine. Life in Daly City was difficult, particularly in the Bay Area in 1978. The cost of living was exorbitant, and despite my position at the hospital, I struggled to make ends meet. Taylor's work volatility exacerbated the stress. We both felt the tension.

In September 1978, Taylor inquired whether I wanted to return to Minnesota. I quickly replied, "Yes." The Bay Area was a challenging location for us, and coming to Minnesota felt like an opportunity for a new beginning. We packed our possessions again and made the transfer.

Back in Minnesota, we hoped to find more stability and a sense of belonging. The familiar surroundings offered some comfort, but the challenges didn't disappear overnight. Taylor struggled to find consistent work, and the pressures of our daily lives weighed heavily on us. As I settled into life in Minnesota, I reflected on how much had changed since the early days of our marriage. The carefree moments seemed like a distant memory. Now, we were grappling with the realities of adult life, trying to make the best of our situation.

Living close to Taylor's family again brought its own set of challenges. The gatherings with cases of beer were a regular occurrence, and I found myself once more trying to fit in and keep the peace. I continued to grab a bottle here and there, using it to cope with the stress and uncertainty of our lives.

Nonetheless, that guarded optimism that everything would be better someday persisted in my mind. I believed that somewhere in Minnesota, a life of stability and happiness awaited us. I refused to give up on this chapter of our life; in a larger sense, I was determined to wade through the hard times for the good of our family.

The years that have since passed since then have made me realize how formative these early events were for me. Every struggle and every trial was yet another test of endurance, another lesson in persevering and remaining steadfast.

Looking back on those years, I am reminded of the incredible strength it took to endure those ups and downs. The resolve was one of hope and sheer determination, which is not the same as a confident belief; however, they underpinned in me the conviction that something better awaited me and our whole family.

Chapter Seven

No Questions Asked

By October 1978, we had moved back to Minnesota and lived with Taylor's grandfather, Patrick, for a few weeks until we found an apartment in Wahpeton, North Dakota. It was uncertain, and everything depended on Taylor finding work first. It seemed that Tom was conflicted about living with his family in the midwest and make our home in the Bay Area. Eventually, he found a job at the beet plant, and we could rent a basement apartment.

When Taylor and I were out of town for his job interviews, I left Chloe with his parents, Tracy and Conrad, and his three younger siblings, Josie, Jacob, and Mateo. Every day when we got back, I brought Chloe home. Those separations were short but difficult, as it was the first time something took me away from my baby.

Between October and December of 1978, it felt like a time of stability. We were getting used to the routine after living in a new place. Years later, I learned that Taylor's mother convinced us to return to Minnesota. I learned she was meddling more with our lives than she should have been allowed.

December 1978 was a difficult month to endure. Taylor came home one day from work with two Christmas presents. The first was a doll with brown hair and brown eyes for Chloe, and the second was a watch for me. He also bought a bottle of whiskey with himself. Once we got those presents, Chloe reacted to the doll in a way I was not expecting. Her eyes widened with fright, and tears started streaming down her face. She sucked on her fingers, with the horrified look still on her face. I took the doll out of the box, hoping it'd make her feel better. She tore the doll's head off with a strange look. She was only 17 months old.

I couldn't understand why she did that, but it stuck with me ever since.

Living in Wahpeton came with its own set of challenges. The small-town atmosphere starkly contrasted with our life in the Bay Area. I missed the vibrancy and opportunities of California, but I tried to make the best of our situation.

After Christmas, Josie stayed with us for a week, sharing Cloe's room. When Tracy came to pick her up, Josie seemed distant and unfriendly. Her presence reminded us of the family dynamics that often strained our lives.

By December 1979, Taylor asked if I would consider moving again. He wanted me to look for work in another area. Opening the local newspaper, the Fargo Forum, I found two nursing job listings in California. The first is in Delano, and the other is in Colusa. I interviewed for both, and Colusa offered a bonus if I moved within two weeks and covered our moving expenses in exchange for two years of service. We decided to go for it.

We drove cross-country in December 1979, arriving in Colusa just before the new year. They put us up in a motel until we found an apartment. By January 1980, I started work at Eskaton Colusa Hospital, and Taylor found a job at the Auction Yard Cafe in Williams.

Those years in Colusa were some of the best in our marriage. Being away from Tracy's incessant intrusion allowed us to breathe and reconnect. Our life settled into a comfortable routine. I was busy with my job at the hospital, and Taylor seemed content with his work at the cafe. We felt like a

normal family for a while, away from the pressures and expectations that had always followed us.

In May 1982, our second daughter, Jenna, was born. The
joy of welcoming a new baby brought us even closer. Cloe
was thrilled to have a little sister, and our home was filled
with happiness after her arrival.

However, the peace was short-lived. In September, we
were summoned to Minnesota because Pete, Taylor's grandfather, wanted to give some money to his grandchildren.
Jenna was still an infant, and the trip was daunting, but I
managed to get time off from work, and Taylor did too.
Tracy's pull was strong, and we again followed her orders.

The visit to Minnesota was another reminder of the control Tracy had over our lives. Despite the distance, her influence was ever-present. The money from Pete was
appreciated, but it came with strings attached, another attempt to pull us back into the fold.

Returning to Colusa, I renewed my determination to
maintain the stability we had found. Yet, the seed of doubt
had been planted. How long could we resist the pull of family obligations and the expectations that came with them?

For now, we are focused on our lives in Colusa. Taylor
and I worked hard to provide a good home for Cloe and
Jenna. Our marriage, though tested by external pressures,
was strong. We had found a rhythm that worked for us, and
I was determined to protect it. As I look back on those years,
I see them as a series of physical and emotional moves. Each
move brought new challenges and opportunities.

The summer of 1983 brought another visit from Parker,
his second time staying with us. He stayed in a motel while
on vacation, which gave us space. One evening, I joined a
conversation between Parker and Taylor while still in my

nightgown. Taylor was furious, his tone bossy, controlling, and punitive. He chastised me for interrupting, making me feel small and insignificant.

Taylor's behavior had grown increasingly oppressive. He watched me intensely in different settings and chastised me if he felt I didn't act appropriately. His controlling nature was becoming unbearable. Whenever I tried to point out his faults or express my discomfort, he always had an excuse, turning the blame back on me.

By September, we decided it was time for another move. My contract at Eskaton Colusa Hospital was up, and Taylor had found work in Oakland as a manager at Fenton's Ice Creamery. He moved to San Francisco first and stayed with my parents while I stayed back in Colusa to pack up our house.

Packing up the house was a daunting task. Every item I put away reminded me of the life we had built there. The memories of our time in Colusa were a mix of good and bad, but they were ours. I was determined to handle the move efficiently, knowing that joining Taylor in San Francisco was the next step we needed to take.

Finally, when everything was packed and ready, I joined Taylor at my parents' house. Reuniting with him felt strange, as if we were starting a new chapter with the same old conflicts lurking in the background. Living with my parents added a layer of complexity.

Taylor's job at Senton's Ice Creamery in Oakland kept him busy. He seemed to thrive in his new role, as he was enjoying the responsibilities, and the change of pace worked for him. I felt a sense of pride for him, but it did not change the fact that there was an underlying tension in our relationship, which persisted. Despite the new role and the job, there was no major effect on his controlling nature. It remained exactly like how it was. Due to this, I struggled to find my footing in this new environment.

I took some time and decided to explore job opportunities in the Bay Area. I needed to find a new job for financial reasons and my sense of independence and self-worth. Although the hunt for a new job proved to be more challenging than I had hoped for, I knew something substantial would come up deep down.

During all this time, I tried to focus on the positive aspects. I focused on things like how much we were closer to family, which provided a support system, and the change of scenery, which offered a fresh perspective. Despite the ongoing challenges with Taylor, I found comfort in the small victories, whether securing a job interview or simply enjoying a peaceful moment in our new home. We faced many challenges, but I was determined to find a way forward. I knew the road ahead wouldn't be easy.

Chapter Eight

Move After Move

In October 1983, we moved into an apartment in Castro Valley. Taylor continued his work at Senton's Ice Creamery while I found work doing private-duty nursing. It was a challenging phase in our lives. We had to balance work and family. But one thing that was going for us was the determination to make it work. At least, I thought we both had that; I am not so sure now.

June 1984, our situation had changed. Things had taken a turn for the better. I had secured a position with the Kaiser Pain Management Program in Hayward, which offered more stability and satisfaction. We resided in Castro Valley from October 1983 until December 1984, and then we bought a house in Hayward. It felt like a huge step forward in our journey. I saw it as a testament to our hard work and perseverance. We were excited about our new home. It was a symbol of a fresh start in our lives.

However, our excitement was short-lived as life happened. One moment, you are on top of the world; the next, you face an unexpected hurdle. Two weeks after we bought the house, Tracy visited, bringing Conrad along. Her visit was ostensibly to see our new home on the surface. But deep down, they had far worse intentions. That visit marked the beginning of her harassment. She scrutinized every detail of the house, her eyes filled with barely concealed jealousy.

Years later, a friend confided in me that her jealousy drove Tracy's quick visit and scrutiny. She couldn't stand the thought of us having something she deemed better or more successful. This revelation shed light on many of her actions and made me realize the depth of her insecurities.

Despite Tracy's challenges, we focused on settling into our new home. Taylor and I worked hard to make it a place of comfort and stability for our family. We were determined not to let Tracy's jealousy and interference overshadow our happiness.

Our time in Hayward was a mix of settling into our new environment and dealing with the lingering pressures from Tracy. But through it all, we remained committed to each other and building a life we could be proud of.

In January 1985, Parker and his friend Tim Nelson visited us. It also felt more like a surveillance mission than a friendly visit. From 1985 until 2018, Tracy harassed us with cards, letters, and calls for over 40 years. Taylor's abusive behavior intensified during this time. I assume Tracy's interference fueled it. She insisted we return to Minnesota regularly, keeping her influence strong.

One night during Parker's visit, I was in the kitchen doing dishes. The girls, then eight and three years old, were supposed to be in bed. I heard a noise from the back of the house and investigated. Taylor and Parker were standing in the hallway near the entrance to Parker's room. When I asked what was happening, Taylor claimed Parker said someone was trying to break into the house. Parker pointed to the French doors, which were partially open, with a chain keeping them from opening further. His sheepish look made me suspicious. I voiced my disbelief to Taylor.

He responded angrily, "Are you calling my brother a liar?"

He blocked the hallway, preventing me from checking the girls' bedroom. With no way to argue, I returned to the kitchen. This incident, like many others, was never discussed again. Taylor's behavior followed a familiar pattern. He would permanently hide something and accuse me of being the problem if I questioned him.

He would say, "You're crazy, you're not satisfied, you're always causing trouble."

Taylor's need to make me wrong to make himself right seemed to stem from deep-seated issues from his earlier years. His controlling nature and the constant meddling from Tracy created a toxic environment.

Balancing work, managing the household, and dealing with Taylor's behavior was exhausting. My job at the Kaiser Pain Management Program provided a sense of stability and independence, but the strain at home was constant. Taylor's controlling nature and Tracy's interference tested my patience and limits.

Throughout these years, I worked hard to shield our daughters from the mayhem. Cloe and Jenna were my priority, and I wanted to provide them with a stable and loving environment. But Taylor's behavior made this aim of mine a daunting task. On one hand, I was trying to create normalcy for them, and on the other hand, Taylor was causing all the chaos. Reflecting on those years, I see a woman who fought tirelessly to maintain her sanity and protect her children. Taylor's abusive behavior and Tracy's incessant meddling were significant hurdles, but I remained steadfast. My job, my daughters, and the small moments of peace and joy kept me going.

Moving forward, I knew that our journey would be filled with challenges. But I was determined to find a way to navigate through them. My strength and resilience would be my guiding light, ensuring our family remained intact despite the odds.

In February 1986, we were summoned back to Minnesota because Pete wasn't doing well. The trip was stressful, as always. By May 1986, Taylor had to return for Pete's funeral, another somber occasion drawing us back to Minnesota.

From 1987 to 1995, life seemed relatively stable. Family life was generally fair, with several visits to and from Minnesota during this period. However, it was always something. Either it was some monumental occasion or something else that dragged us back. I went along with these visits, though I didn't enjoy them. By then, I was constantly on guard, watching for situations that didn't feel right or caused me to hesitate. The odd turn of events triggered me. Additionally, the constant need to agree to plans I didn't fully support agitated me greatly and weighed heavily on me.

In 1990 or 1991, we traveled to Minnesota for a wedding. It was Minnie and Jacob's. All these trips were always a mix of obligatory family gatherings and underlying tension. Despite the burden, I always did my best to maintain a semblance of normalcy for the sake of our family.

In 1996, a shadow fell over my life when my doctors informed me that I had uterine fibroids. I was already under a lot of stress at work and home, so the diagnosis came as a huge blow. The walls seemed to be closing in around me. The phrase "uterine fibroids" echoed as I sat in the chilly clinical doctor's office, pushing everything else aside.

I was overcome with a sensation of unease and terror. The emotional toll was as significant as the physical agony. I was frightened about having surgery or other intrusive procedures. My head was filled with inquiries: How would this affect my health? How would I manage work and family during this time? Would Taylor be supportive, or would his controlling nature make things even more complicated?

Taylor's response was expected. He downplayed my worries, saying I was exaggerating and it wasn't a huge problem. His lack of compassion was profound. I felt isolated, unable to get the much-needed emotional support while I dealt with my health issue. It was another reminder of the emotional gulf that grew between us yearly.

During this chaos, I was drawn to holistic medicine and wellness. It was a semblance of power and optimism, a lifeline. I started looking at alternative therapies to address my illness organically. This route toward holistic health became more than simply a means of managing my fibroids; it was also a means of regaining my autonomy and sense of self.

I started incorporating small changes into my daily routine—herbal teas, yoga, meditation. Each practice was a step towards healing, not just my body but my spirit. These moments of self-care became sacred, a refuge from the chaos of my life. I found strength in these practices, a quiet resilience that helped me face each day.

The girls noticed the changes, too. Cloe and Jenna saw me taking time for myself and prioritizing my health. It wasn't just about the physical treatments but setting an example for them. I wanted them to see that it was okay to take care of themselves and seek balance and well-being in a world that often demanded too much.

As I embraced holistic health, I also began to see my situation with clearer eyes. I started to understand the toxic dynamics in my marriage and the ways Tracy's influence had permeated our lives. This newfound clarity gave me the courage to set boundaries to push back against the constant demands and manipulations.

There were still many obstacles to overcome, and recovery

was not easy. But I sensed a ray of optimism for the first time in a long time. I was taking charge of my life and health and was resolved to find a way to go forward, no matter how challenging the path may be.

This path toward self-care and holistic wellness was life-changing. It was evidence of my tenacity and unshakable will to improve my and my girls' lives. Despite the difficulties, I took comfort in the little triumphs and the moments of empowerment and serenity that accompanied each step toward recovery.

Chapter Nine

Minnesota: The Switching Point

In 1997, we made another trip to Minnesota, a journey that always filled me with dread and resignation. Despite our frequent visits, we stayed at Tracy and Conrad's farmhouse, which never felt like home to me. Taylor and Jenna spent their days in the fields, where he was teaching her how to shoot a rifle. It was one of the few activities they seemed to bond over. Tracy stayed inside, managing the household with her usual stern efficiency.

One afternoon, I went to look for Cloe, who had wandered off to Parker's trailer. I knocked on the door and stepped inside, finding Cloe and Parker sitting on a high counter, playing a penny game. They both looked perturbed by my presence, their expressions making it clear I had interrupted something. As I glanced around the trailer, my eyes were drawn to a classic Singer sewing machine that had belonged to their grandmother. It was a beautiful antique, a piece of the family's history that intrigued me.

I pulled open a drawer on the sewing machine out of sheer curiosity. I opened it to see a tiny box with a buttonhole maker and a short pamphlet with handwritten directions on stitching a buttonhole. The note was charming and personal, a piece of the past that I thought would be wonderful to pass down to one of my daughters. It seemed like a lovely keepsake that connected us to previous generations. I asked Parker if I could have it, hoping for a moment of family generosity.

"No!" Parker responded angrily to my innocent request.

His reaction was sharp and hostile, a stark reminder of Taylor's family's unwelcoming and possessive nature. It was disheartening. I had only wanted to preserve a piece of family history for my girls, but sharing was not in their nature.

During our visits, I always felt a profound sense of separation, both mentally and physically. My children slept in the attic area, away from the rest of the family. The grandparents occupied the first floor, while Taylor and I slept in the front room on the same floor. The physical distance within the house mirrored my emotional distance from Taylor's family. I chose to have the girls sleep in the attic because I was concerned about potential impropriety from Taylor's family members. I wanted to ensure their safety and peace of mind.

Each visit to Minnesota reinforced my feelings of isolation and unease. The house, though familiar, never felt like a place where I belonged. Taylor's family's lack of warmth and generosity left me constantly on edge. I had to deal with their coldness and protect my daughters from the toxic environment that pervaded the household.

Living in Taylor's family's house was a stark reminder of the underlying issues that plagued our relationship and my place within his family. The lack of warmth, generosity, and constant need to protect my daughters left me feeling more alienated with each visit. But I held onto my resolve, determined to navigate these complex family dynamics while safeguarding the happiness and safety of my children.

These trips were always fraught with tension and discomfort. Despite the scenic setting of the farm and the activities that kept Taylor and Jenna busy, I couldn't shake the feeling of being an outsider. The cold interactions, the dismissive attitudes, and the blatant favoritism shown to other family members were hard to ignore.

My determination to protect Cloe and Jenna never wavered. I made sure they were safe and away from any potential harm. My vigilance was a silent rebellion against the oppressive atmosphere that Tracy and her family perpetuated. I was their shield, the barrier between my daughters and the dysfunction that threatened to engulf us.

Despite the challenges, I found comfort in the small acts of defiance—like my attempt to claim a piece of family history for my girls. Though often met with resistance, each of these acts reinforced my resolve to carve out a space for us, a place where we could feel safe and valued.

These visits constantly reminded me of the resilience required to maintain my sense of self and protect my family. I faced each trip with dread and determination, knowing the path ahead was difficult. But in those moments of quiet strength, I found the courage to continue, fight for my daughter's well-being and happiness, and hold onto the hope that we would someday find a place where we truly belonged.

In May 1998, I decided to send Taylor to Minnesota for a birthday gift. I hoped the trip would provide him with some much-needed relaxation and a chance to reconnect with his roots. However, when Taylor returned, it was like he had returned a dark cloud. When he stepped off the plane, he was irritable and distant, his behavior erratic and unpredictable. This change lingered for the rest of the year, casting a pall over our home and leaving me to wonder what had happened during his visit.

October 1998 brought another devastating blow: my father passed away. The grief was overwhelming, and amid this sorrow, my mother needed a place to stay. We got her into our home until we could arrange for senior housing.

This period should have been a time of family coming together, of support and healing. Instead, it was clouded by Taylor's anger and resentment. He was furious about my mother's presence in our home, his lack of empathy and compassion a painful contrast to the care and concern I felt for her.

Taylor's anger during this transition was palpable. He resented the attention and care my mother required, viewing her presence as an intrusion rather than a necessity born of compassion and familial duty. From October through January, our household was in constant turmoil. Taylor's needs and demands overshadowed everything else. He insisted that his needs were paramount, disregarding the fact that my mother was grieving and vulnerable. His selfishness was heartbreaking, adding to the stress and emotional strain I was already experiencing.

I was pushed to my absolute maximum at this moment. I was taking care of my mother, grieving for my father, trying to keep things as normal as possible for Cloe and Jenna, and putting up with Taylor's growing hatred. There was a tremendous emotional cost. I felt like I was always treading carefully as I tried to control Taylor's tantrums and provide my family stability and support. It seemed like a fight inside the house that ought to have been a haven.

In December 1998, the situation reached a breaking point. In frustration and anger, Taylor threatened to leave me and visit his friend Bruce in Washington State. His timing could not have been worse. I was already struggling to keep everything together, and his threat to abandon us when I needed him most felt like a profound betrayal. His desire to escape and avoid responsibility highlighted the growing chasm between us. His threats made it clear that he saw himself as the victim, incapable of offering support when it was most needed.

Taylor's behavior during this period underscored the depth of our challenges. His controlling nature and lack of empathy were exacerbated by the constant interference from his family, particularly Tracy. I often felt isolated and un-supported, left to navigate these difficult situations inde-pendently. Despite these challenges, I focused on my role as a mother and a daughter. My mother's presence reminded me of the strength and resilience I had inherited from her, and I was determined to provide the same support and sta-bility for Cloe and Jenna.

Throughout these months, I clung to the hope that things would eventually improve. I sought solace in my holistic health practices, finding brief reprieves in meditation, herbal teas, and yoga. These practices were lifelines, offering me moments of peace amidst the chaos. But even these mo-ments of self-care often felt insufficient against the relentless storm within our home.

My priorities became more apparent as I made my way through this trying time. Even if it meant defying Taylor and his irrational demands, I was determined to keep my girls safe and offer them a stable home. My mother's presence turned from being a cause of conflict to one of strength. She served as a reminder of the value of family and the necessity of supporting one another during trying times.

In my life, these events in 1998 were a major turning point. They brought to light the difficulties of cohabiting with an authoritarian and unsupportive spouse, but they also brought attention to my resilience and empathy. De-spite the challenges, I managed to take care of my kids, help my mother, and be true to who I was. Every hardship was evidence of my fortitude and a reminder of the unwavering spirit that propelled me ahead in the face of difficulty.

In retrospect, these months were a testing ground, a period of extreme stress and change. They made me face the truth of my circumstances and muster the courage to defend my family and myself. The enormous obstacles I faced in 1998 also served as a mirror for my inner fortitude and resolve. I came out of the darkness with a stronger purpose and a better comprehension of my resilience.

Chapter Ten

"Yes, I Am A Big Girl!"

In February 1999, Valentine's Day weekend was marred by a visit from Taylor's brothers, Parker and Jacob, and Jacob's wife, Minnie. They stayed at the Hyatt Regency near the San Francisco airport, foreshadowing the uncomfortable dynamics of the visit. Minnie, who worked at Creative Memory, was notably cold towards me and flirtatious with Taylor. Her behavior was inappropriate and hurtful. During their stay, Taylor's simmering anger towards me overshadowed the weekend.

On Thursday, we took them to one of our favorite restaurants in San Francisco. The dinner should have been a pleasant family gathering, but instead, I found myself increasingly excluded from the conversation. The talk was directed primarily at Taylor, and I felt invisible. When the dinner ended, I wanted to leave an extra tip for the staff, a small gesture of gratitude. As I moved to do so, Minnie sharply informed me that she had already taken care of the bill. Taylor's silence in the face of her rudeness was a painful reminder of his lack of support. His indifference was like a knife to my heart, reinforcing the loneliness I felt within my marriage.

June 1999 was supposed to be a time of celebration and joy as my mother reached the remarkable milestone of her 85th birthday. We planned an unforgettable trip to Ireland and France to mark the occasion. The trip was designed to be a bonding experience, an opportunity for my daughters and me to create lasting memories with my mother. But from the very beginning, Cloe's behavior casts a pall over the journey. She seemed reluctant and distant, her actions filled with a silent resistance I couldn't understand.

Cloe's reluctance to fully engage in the trip was disheartening. Despite the breathtaking landscapes of Ireland and the rich cultural history of France, her mood was indifferent, almost as if she resented being there. Jenna, always protective of her older sister, mirrored Cloe's behavior, adding to the tension. I tried to cater to Cloe, hoping to soothe whatever was troubling her. I was constantly on edge, trying to ensure everyone enjoyed themselves, but the strain was evident. The palpable distance between us overshadowed the joy I had hoped to feel on this special trip.

A year later, in June 2000, we made another journey to Minnesota for our niece Janice's wedding. We stayed at a resort, hoping for a brief respite from our everyday stresses. However, the trip was anything but relaxing. As soon as we arrived, Taylor's parents, Tracy and Conrad, demanded his help on the farm. This demand was familiar, as they often kept him busy with tasks, isolating him from me and the children. It was as though they were determined to keep him under their control.

Taylor's anger towards me during this trip was intense and relentless. His frustration at being pulled away to work on the farm translated into harsh words and cold silences directed at me. This recurring pattern of behavior had become a hallmark of our visits to Minnesota, and it wore heavily on my spirit. My sister-in-law Lisa noticed the manipulation, remembering how Tracy and Conrad deliberately kept Taylor and Arthur apart. The tension during our stay was unbearable, and once again, I felt like an outsider in my own family.

June 2001 marked another significant family event – Taylor's parents' 50th wedding anniversary. Taylor traveled to Minnesota alone for the celebration, and his parents visited us afterward. This visit was particularly tense because, before their arrival, I had finally confronted Tracy over the phone about her years of mistreatment. The confrontation had been a long time coming, and though it was liberating to voice my grievances, it also set the stage for an incredibly tense visit.

When Tracy and Conrad arrived, the atmosphere in our home was thick with unspoken animosity. Cloe's behavior continued to be odd, reflecting the ongoing turmoil within our family. She was distant and aloof, her actions adding to the overall tension. During this visit, I was acutely aware of the years of abuse and neglect I had endured. I realized that I could no longer stay silent.

These experiences culminated in a significant turning point in my life. I began to stand up for myself, driven by a growing defiance against the years of emotional abuse and neglect. I decided to quit trying to appease everyone at my expense. When Tracy and Conrad visited in June 2001, I finally confronted Tracy in person. I expressed my feelings about her years of mistreatment, a confrontation that had been brewing for years. It was liberating to voice my grievances, even if it didn't change the dynamics immediately.

On my 26th anniversary of marriage, I reached the realization with bitterness. Taylor's actions on our anniversary weekend highlighted the increasing distance between us and demonstrated his increasing control over our lives. I felt like I was married to a stranger even though I had been married for over 20 years. When I voiced my complaints about his lack of support, he said, "You're a big girl and besides you are married to me," which reminded me of his emotional detachment and lack of empathy.

My decision to stand up to Taylor and his family largely facilitated my regaining independence. It wasn't simple, and there were severe, fast consequences. However, I realized that I had sacrificed my pleasure and well-being for maintaining peace for far too long. It was time to put my needs first and safeguard my mental well-being.

The culmination of these events and the realizations they brought about led to a moment of profound clarity. I understood that my worth was not defined by Taylor's approval or his family's acceptance. I was a big girl, and it was time to start living for myself. This chapter of defiance was just the beginning of a long journey towards self-discovery and empowerment. Despite the hardships, I emerged stronger, ready to face whatever lay ahead with a renewed sense of purpose and determination.

Our wedding anniversary should have been filled with love and celebration. Instead, it was yet another example of the growing chasm between Taylor and me. The day started with a phone call from Taylor's mother. She and Taylor talked for a while, and when it was my turn to speak with her, I foolishly mentioned our plans to visit Sacramento the next day. Her voice was resentful, a tone I had become all too familiar with. When Taylor returned the phone, I could sense the shift in his demeanor. It was as if a cloud had descended over him, a stupor that always seemed to follow conversations with his mother.

Our trip to Sacramento felt strained and uncomfortable. Taylor was preoccupied, his mind elsewhere. We stopped at The Embassy Suites, but Taylor refused to stay overnight because it cost $130.00. His refusal to spend money on our anniversary weekend stung deeply. It was another reminder of his control over our lives and his lack of regard for my feelings. On the drive back, my frustration boiled over. I was upset and made my feelings known. Sensing my anger, Taylor decided to stop in Williams, and we stayed at the Holiday Inn Express.

As we checked in, Taylor turned to me and said, "I know you hate me." His words cut deep, but I replied honestly, "I don't hate you, I don't understand you." We spent the night there, a stark reminder of how disconnected we had become. The following day, we returned home, and the anniversary weekend was a painful reminder of Taylor's control over our lives. He was not truly married to me while I was married to him.

In August 2009, Taylor and I traveled again to Minnesota for Mateo's wedding. The visit was tense, as always, when we were around Taylor's family. I decided to take this opportunity to speak with his family about how they treated me. It was a difficult and emotionally charged conversation. I expressed my feelings about the years of mistreatment and the lack of support I felt from them.

The responses I received were defensive and dismissive. Tracy, in particular, deflected any blame quickly, insisting that I was causing trouble. She even went so far as to say, "You're an only child; you don't know about family. You are the cause of all the trouble in this family." Her words were like a dagger, highlighting the deep-seated resentment and hatred that had plagued our relationship from the beginning.

It was a big step for me to address Taylor's family, even with the negative responses. After years of quiet, it was a defiant act that I did to defend my rights. Even if nothing changed immediately, the encounter was a vital turning point for empowerment. I concluded that I could not let their abuse dictate who I was going to be. No matter the cost, I had to prioritize my health and advocate for myself.

2002 and 2009 played a crucial role in my quest for empowerment. Every argument, every act of rebellion, was a step toward recovering my own will. I realized my value was independent of Taylor's or his family's acceptance. Their attempts to subjugate and control me made me more determined to resist their hold over me.

Realizing I could advocate for myself as a "big girl" seemed freeing and intimidating. I would no longer be defined by the needs and expectations of others, and a new chapter in my life started. I began to regard myself as a powerful, self-reliant woman worthy of admiration and affection.

As I reflected on the years of emotional turmoil and abuse, I found a renewed sense of purpose. I embraced my strength and resilience, determined to create a life that was true to myself. This journey was difficult, with many moments of doubt and fear. But with each step, I grew more confident in my ability to navigate the challenges that lay ahead.

From my experiences, I learned how important it is to take charge of one's life and advocate for oneself. It dawned on me that I had been sacrificing my happiness and well-being for other people's enjoyment for far too long. It was time to put my needs first and safeguard my mental well-being.

Chapter Eleven

Patterns Of Emotional Neglect, Abuse, And Control

Due to Taylor's alcoholism and abusive energy, which has become a family disease, we have all been affected through the years in many different ways. Everyone's unpredictable moods made home life a constant battle. I felt like I was walking on eggshells, never knowing when the next conflict would erupt.

By 2017, the tension within our family had reached a boiling point. In March of that year, we traveled to Minnesota for Conrad's funeral. The trip was fraught with emotional landmines. Cloe and Jenna's odd behavior towards me persisted, amplifying my sense of alienation. Despite being surrounded by family, I was profoundly alone.

***

Amid these family upheavals, Taylor received a diagnosis of Parkinson's disease. This diagnosis, instead of bringing us closer, drove an even deeper wedge between us. Taylor's control over me intensified, and his behavior became more erratic and abusive. His drinking escalated, and his verbal abuse became a daily ordeal. The man I had married seemed to be disappearing, replaced by a stranger consumed by anger and alcoholism.

I also began to suspect that Taylor was struggling with his sexuality. His behavior and how he interacted with certain men raised questions I couldn't ignore. Although I had no definitive proof, my suspicions gnawed at me. I felt he was unable to come out of the closet, trapped by societal and familial expectations. This added another layer of complexity to our already strained relationship.

**

As I thought back on our marriage throughout the years, I noticed a pattern of emotional neglect, abuse, and control. This dynamic was greatly influenced by Taylor's family, especially his mother. Taylor's hatred and bitterness towards me remained unabated due to her constant bombardment of messages, letters, and photos. Her meddling was a constant force that strained our union. Taylor's mother's constant interference destroyed our bridge, brick by brick, no matter how hard I tried to mend it.

Taylor's actions reminded me painfully of my father's behavior, which took me back to my early years. His hostility, verbal assaults, and accusations of infidelity mirrored the problems I had intended to leave behind. Rather than discovering the affection and assistance I so desperately needed, I discovered myself imprisoned in an all too familiar pattern of abuse. Having doubts about Taylor's sexual orientation simply made me feel more alone and betrayed. My life partner, whom I had trusted, was harboring secrets that erected an impenetrable barrier between us that caused our marriage to fail. Taylor's mother's constant interference destroyed our bridge, brick by brick, no matter how hard I tried to mend it.

My kids took on a harsh and aloof attitude because of Taylor's anger, alcoholism, and Parkinson's Disease. They were just as callous and indifferent to me as Taylor had been.

Their opinion of me thwarted my attempt to build a loving relationship with Cloe and Jenna as an outsider in our family. Our marriage had no feeling of cooperation left after Taylor's violence and control. It seemed like I had no allies and was fighting a war on several fronts. Instead of being a haven, my house became a battlefield where I was outnumbered and outmatched.

This was a difficult and profound time in my life. It was a time of great emotional strain but also a time of development and fortitude. I had to face the painful realities of my marriage and my resilience after every setback. After going through these events, I better appreciated my strengths and a fresh resolve to live authentically. My experiences taught me the value of self-respect and how valuable I am. I take the knowledge I've gained and my steadfast faith in my capacity to triumph over hardship as I look to the future. My past experiences have made me stronger and more resilient, and I'm prepared to confront any obstacles with bravery and tenacity.

In looking at life and relationships, there is a fine quote by Shakespeare that states: *"Oh what a tangled web we weave when first we practice to deceive."* I want to add to this quote with my own saying: *"The deception of the Self is the most painful one of them all."*

Chapter Twelve

"I Am All I Have"

Thanksgiving Day, 2019, began a significant turning point. I took charge, as both Taylor's wife and the mother of our children, determined to care for him and manage the household. I wanted Cloe and Jenna to live their lives without the burden of constant worry. They deserved some semblance of normalcy amidst the chaos. However, the reality was far from what I hoped for.

The final chapter of Taylor's life was fraught with emotional and physical turmoil. The first rush to the hospital was a stark wake-up call. Taylor's health had been declining, and despite his earlier Parkinson's diagnosis, it was now clear that there was more at play. The doctors soon confirmed our worst fears: Taylor had cancer. The diagnosis was like a shadow descending over our lives, bringing with it a sense of dread and inevitability.

Taylor's inability to accept his true self manifested in anger and abuse towards me. It was a tragic cycle of self-loathing projected onto others. My analysis of our marriage reveals a painful truth: Taylor's struggle with his identity and the lies he lived was at the heart of our dysfunctional relationship.

To all the readers who have journeyed with me through these pages, my story is about resilience and self-discovery. It is a testimony to the strength within us, even when we feel isolated and unsupported. The deception of oneself is the worst kind of deceit, and breaking free from that is the first step towards true liberation.

As time went on, I came to understand that I was everything. It took me decades to realize that neither Taylor's nor his family's acceptance determined my value. I ought to have acknowledged my strength and defended myself earlier. Although I used my quiet as a coping strategy, it also let the abuse go undetected. It became a pivotal moment when I realized that all I had was myself. I had to have a painful but necessary awakening before truly accepting my worth.

For a very long time, I thought that by being silent and not stirring up any trouble, I was the appropriate parent to my family. I mistakenly believed that bearing the suffering in silence demonstrated strength, but it was a shackle. This quiet did not shield me or my girls; rather, it served to maintain the abusive and controlling dynamic. Years of pain and suffering later, I realized how important it was to stand up for myself to escape the poisonous atmosphere that had held me for so long.

To sum up, my path has involved both suffering and development. My experiences have taught me the value of self-determination and the necessity of speaking up against injustice, especially in one's own family. Although maintaining silence might seem like a good idea, it frequently worsens the same suffering we want to stop. The path to healing and emancipation eventually lies in having the guts to stand up and declare one's value. I hope that those who have experienced comparable hardships can relate to my story and be motivated to speak up for themselves.

"I was all I had and should have owned it."

This sentence sums up my journey's main points. It appeals to everybody who feels excluded or alone. Accept your value, be strong, and never allow someone to make you feel less than they are. You are the one who defines your journey and can mold it into one of resiliency and success. Never forget that you have an inner power that can get you through even the worst moments, despite how alone you may feel.

To those who feel imprisoned in their quiet, remember that you have a strong voice. Although speaking out might be intimidating, doing so is essential to taking back your life and establishing your worth. It's a path toward self-acceptance and liberation but also calls for a great deal of guts. Realizing you have the inner power to triumph over hardship is the first step toward living a happy and peaceful life.

In retrospect, I see that the goal of my trip was to thrive against all difficulties, not merely to survive. Every obstacle I faced and every depressing moment I had helped me become a better, more confident version of myself. By telling my experience, I want to help anyone with trouble by illuminating their path and demonstrating that overcoming obstacles is possible, discovering your voice, and standing firmly in your truth.

So, have heart, everyone who reads these words. Your strength is greater than you may think; you are not alone. Accept your path, take responsibility for your reality, and never forget you can build a resilient and successful life.

As I reflected on the years of emotional turmoil and abuse, I found a renewed sense of purpose. I embraced my strength and resilience, determined to create a life that was true to myself. This journey was difficult, with many moments of doubt and fear. But with each step, I grew more confident in my ability to navigate the challenges that lay ahead.

From my experiences, I learned how important it is to take charge of one's life and advocate for oneself. It dawned on me that I had been sacrificing my happiness and well-being for other people's enjoyment for far too long. It was time to put my needs first and safeguard my mental well-being.

ABOOKS

ALIVE Book Publishing and ALIVE Publishing Group
are imprints of Advanced Publishing LLC,
3200 A Danville Blvd., Suite 204, Alamo, California 94507

Telephone: 925.837.7303
alivebookpublishing.com

9 781631 322600